Carmina Masoliver is a poet fr
of She Grrrowls feminist arts nig
Poetry Café and has been featur
Fringe and Women of the Worl
was published by Nasty Little
the She Grrrowls anthology, also from Burning Eye Books. She was long-listed for the Young Poet Laureate for London award in 2013, the inaugural Jerwood Compton Poetry Fellowships in 2017, and for the Out-Spoken Prize in Performance Poetry 2018. Alumni of the Roundhouse Poetry Collective, she has featured at nights such as Bang Said the Gun, and festivals including Latitude, Bestival and Lovebox both as a collective and individually. She performed internationally whilst living abroad, in Singapore, and in Spain. Having previously completed an art foundation diploma at Central Saint Martins prior to studying English Literature at UEA, this is her first publication including her own illustrations alongside her poetry

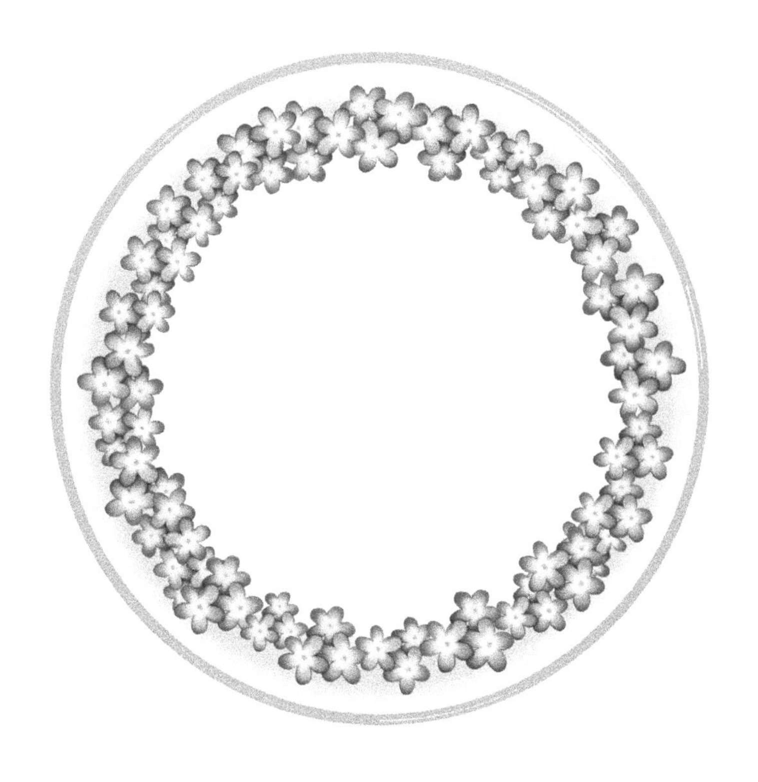

Carmina Masoliver

Burning Eye

This edition published by Burning Eye Books 2019

www.burningeye.co.uk

@burningeyebooks

Burning Eye Books
15 West Hill, Portishead, BS20 6LG

ISBN 978-1-911570-79-0

Circles

To the past, forget me not

I could fall in love again.
I could do this all over again.
But what does that matter?
What does it matter when I love her?

My face cold and pale,
I levitate above my bed
to feel the empty space surround me.
Why do I always see you when I'm ill?
I close my eyes
and I feel the faint warmth of your body like fever.

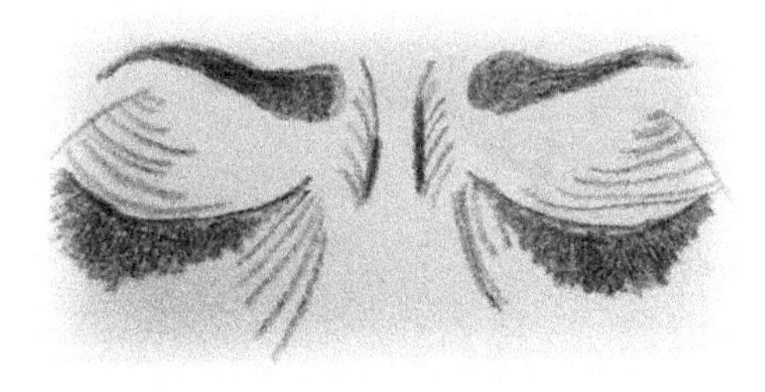

I have met strangers sat on fences.
They claimed to love me
but I just blew them away with the smoke from my cigarette.

I ran away into the shower
and it sang to me, then laughed at me
as it took away the water,
and I joined in
because there is not much else you can do
when a shower head is mocking you in your nakedness.

I am water.
As I wash my hair
it hangs down
and drip
drip
drips
and I become soluble
in the room
which is all dripping.

The mirrors crash to the ground
like sea waves hitting sandy bays.

You left me.
You left me standing in a tangle of long grass,
so far away and small.

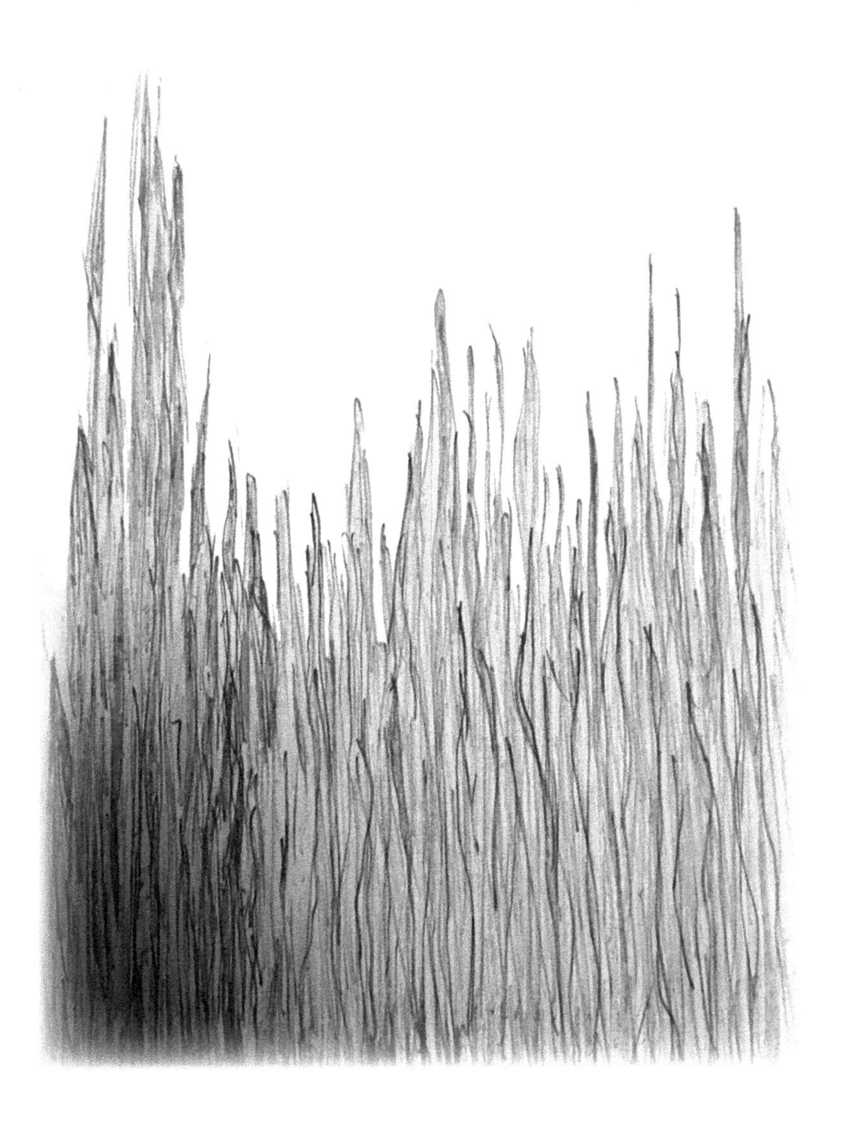

I will become a simple strand of grass,
blowing in the wind as it rushes by the fields
like thin glass mirrors of green,
reflecting one another;
I blend into insignificance.

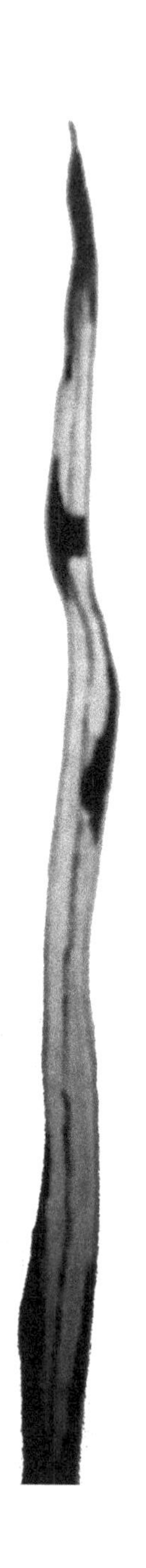

I step out of the shower, towel-turban hair,
dry my body, pull on my underwear,
prepare my mind for another day at work,
button up a clean shirt, slide on a floor-strewn skirt.

A quick slick of make-up, blast of hairdryer, few bites of toast,
and I'm out the door like everything's okay.

I make my way through a web of trains;
like salmon, I swim through a crowd of bodies,
all sweltering in their outdoor coats.

Jump on the Circle line at Westminster for a couple of stops:
a space where I can breathe.

In my periphery, I see a woman
with hair as dark as yours;
it cups her face in that same
smooth curve around her chin.
I take a deep breath in
as I check, inspect, her face.
God is playing some sick joke; she's you,
wearing a mask like a Halloween costume.

I want to whisper,
Sarah, Sarah, take that mask off, you're being cruel,
but I realise I recognise nothing in her eyes.
I tell myself to face the facts;
you are gone, never coming back.

But she's a person.
She's got a face and eyes and skin and a heart and a head and a smile.
I dream, remember, the smell of her hair,
the touch of her body, always warmer than my own,
and the way our eyes would meet, it would feel like home.

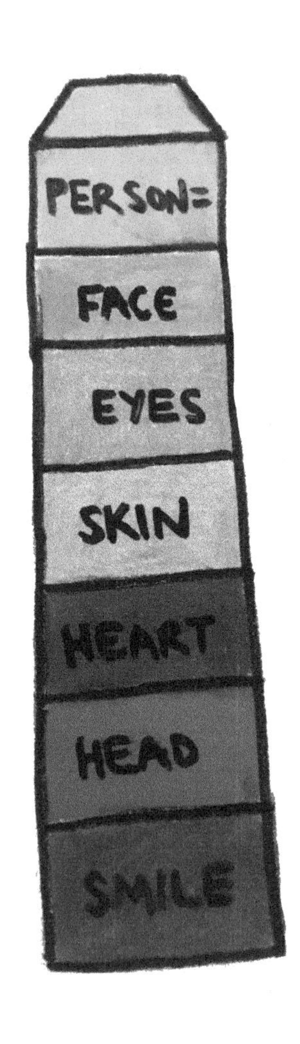

Flash. Flicker. Neon letters speak out:
the next station is Victoria.

We would take our bikes out on summer weekends,
tire ourselves riding through Thorndon Park;
went so fast, it was like we were flying.

Facing the clouds,
I'd turn on my side to see you squinting up at the sky,
scrunching your nose up as you spoke to me until sunset.
You made me laugh until my stomach hurt;
so strange how you made
the darkest thoughts seem funny.

Sometimes we'd stay out so late, we'd be left
staring at the stars,
not even hungry,
feeling so far away.

Flash. Flicker. Neon letters speak out:
the next station is South Kensington.

The carriage slows to a halt. I think, *It's all my fault –*
I've stopped across from an advert
for a bottle of blue WKD,
makes me want to be sick, makes me think…

about the other day, I got asked to dance
by a faceless stranger
as the ground glittered with broken glass
and I pretended things were the same.
Said, *Thanks, but I'm with someone.*

One girl wanted to get all Katy Perry on me.
Bit on her red lipstick lips, all seductive-like.
Told her, *Sorry, not my type*.

A boy who wants to fly in the air
and drop bombs on our planet
judged me by the flowered pattern on my dress.
Hate to say he had me down to a tee. You.
I thought you were the only one who really knew me.
He said he'd been rowing down the Thames that day.
I didn't know what else to say.
My mind was sinking in a drunken haze.

Another bloke was looking over,
got his mate to ask if I was a lesbian.
Told him he should ask himself
if he was so bloody interested.

Didn't want to give him the satisfaction.

I'm not trying to make you jealous.
I'm just trying to make you come back.

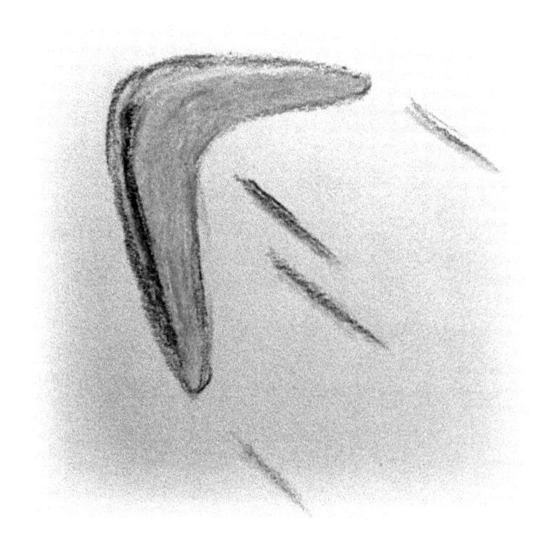

These people, I talk to out of politeness,
and every second
between each breath,
that space between each word they say
when they gulp some air,
I think of you.

3...

I still vomit into dustbins,
blame it on the leather car seats in the taxi,
yet I'm the one with the proper job now,
pretending to be a grown-up.
How is that fair?

When the monotony of tubes and train lines,
phone calls and deadlines, is over,
I've got to get through another weekend
with you gone.

Friends will want to see me, see how I am,
and how can I think up an excuse without you?

There are some memories it is easy to pass by.

You, pacing the room,
your steps hitting the linoleum floor
like a ticking clock on overdrive,
repeating, *I can't go out, I can't go out,*
while, all dressed up, I'd frown and ask,
What are you on about?

You'd say they think you're a crazy bitch,
just like your mum.
I'd reassure you they didn't, but still you
wouldn't come.
I'd argue with you,
but it would be an endless battle.

Then I'd get you to finally sit down,
we'd apologise in unison and I'd say it's okay,
I'd let our friends know we won't be able to go.
I'd tell you they understood,
not mention how they moaned,
how it was directed at you.

Instead, I'd cradle you in my arms,
as you'd rock yourself and cry.
Again and again, how you'd apologise.

So, others wanted to ask me
how I had faith in you.
Because I was sure
you were going to come through
– I'd say,
It's the mindless that say you're doomed.
You're stronger than the others; this is just testing you.

Flash. Flicker. Neon letters speak out:
the next station is Edgware Road.

But she's a person.
She's got a face and eyes and skin and a heart and a head and a smile.
I dream, remember, the smell of her hair,
the touch of her body, always warmer than my own,
and the way our eyes would meet, it would feel like home.

She's got a face
and eyes
and skin
and a heart
and a head
and a smile.

She's got a head,
but her brain
betrays her.
Her mind
is a minefield
          and I never know
                    when the next explosion will be.

But I said I was willing to learn the patterns,
be her anchor, her hot air balloon;
fly with her like kites in the wind.

She said she felt like a puppet.
Strings.
Endless strings.
Got to cut, cut, cut.
Whether apron strings or violins.

I still want her close to me, physically.
We've already got the metaphors;
I want her in the city, pressed up against me in the tube.

We look to Ross and Rachel for affirmation,
not realising they're just a modern fairytale,
still hoping for that happy ever after,
but don't you know that you can never predict disaster?

at the beginning of time
we were one

a moon-made cartwheel with four legs, four arms
and a face like a tragicomedy mask
moulded into a monster through divine eyes

split with a stroke of light

so now laughter exists as a distant echo
in search of half a human
damned by this desire

a hollow cry
through a tunnel with no light

But you were my light.

Flash. Flicker. Neon letters speak out:
the next station is Farringdon.

So, she left me.
Left the city, left the maze of tube trains.
I was holding on to her hand in a reverie,
only to realise it was cold, plastic.
Hanging on to this yellow pole so I don't fall.

She left me, left the city, left the earth.

Yesterday I spoke to her about my day,
but she was already gone.

I sat watching Friends on E4, 'The Last One'
– you know, where *they* get back together –
eating one of those 2-for-1 Indian ready meals we used to get,
amazed at how delicious they were, not cheap-tasting at all.

The second one still in the fridge,
I remembered how we'd lie together after,
our bellies full, her body encasing mine.
I'd try to read her face in the reflection on the television screen.
I was happiest in those times, in her arms.

Now I'm hoping for a heaven where we can meet.
A space where mind and body make no sense,
just souls
awaiting.

Flash. Flicker. Neon letters speak out:
the next station is Liverpool Street.

I hope for a day I will be reunited with my mate.
A sky of stars where we make our own constellation.

I stare into the dark abyss,
searching for messages in the starlight.

You said you felt like I did not exist, but I forgive you.
I will believe in you until I die, then I dare you to prove to
me you're gone.

Prove to me you don't exist
because I cannot believe the so-called reality.

The harsh light of a fresh morning
without you.
The stark contrast of my memories.
I speak and the only voice I want to hear is yours.

The guilt swallows me.
When you said I did not exist,
maybe I could not see what you really meant.

Darling, why did you always have to speak in metaphors?

I wasn't there for you when you wanted to destroy everything.
If only I knew what you were capable of
with prescription drugs, a knife and a handful of rope.

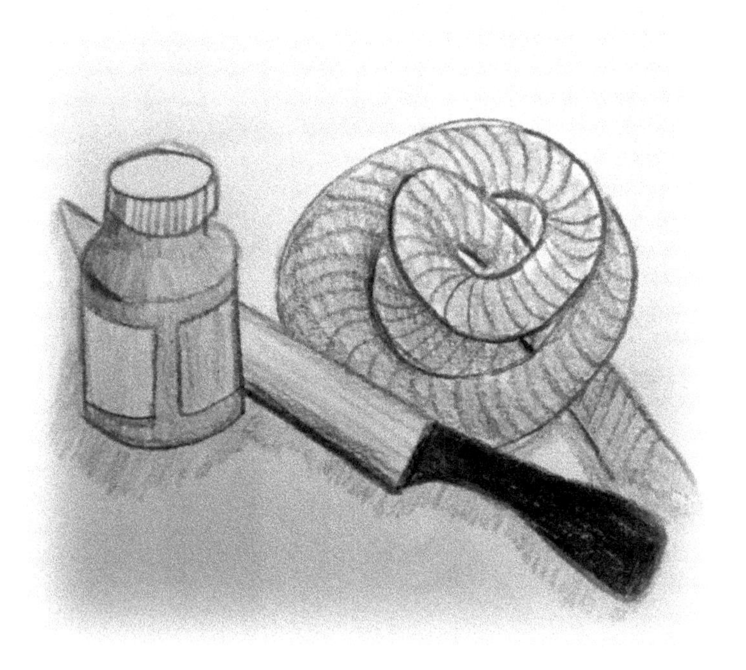

The irony of your bottles of antidepressants
in the bathroom cabinet,
so casually standing next to face cleanser and moisturiser.

I'll never forget the first time you told me you'd love me forever.
I couldn't stop smiling that day, as I watched you,
making the bed, brushing your teeth, getting breakfast,
just like any other day, but not.
Different, because I knew I had your love forever.

If only I knew your version of forever was not the same as mine.

Now I'm left alone
with relics from our past,
left with a finite future.
Promises written in cards,
in ink, permanent;
they masquerade as lies
and I have to believe them
because they are all I have of you.

My love, always.
Sarah

My mind is divided, my body severed from yours.
I will look into the stars tonight and know you're there.

You are the warmth that follows after a shiver down my back,
the wind blowing in my hair as I ride my bike,
the unexplained creaking of floorboards as I eat TV dinners,
the sorrow of a lone magpie, awaiting another life.

Flash. Flicker. Neon letters speak out:
the next station is Victoria.

I step out onto the platform, half hoping I slip into the gap
and seep into the tracks, hide underground with the rats,
but instead I rack my mind,
trying to find a reason to explain why
I rode the Circle line around after missing my stop,
instead of getting off
and getting a tube in the other direction.

'Cause they say
I could fall in love again.
I could do this all over again.
But what does that matter?
What does it matter when I love her?

ACKNOWLEDGEMENTS

Circles is an epic poem created through Apples and Snakes' The Word's a Stage, led by Malika Booker, in 2012. The piece was inspired by Sarah Kane's *4.48 Psychosis*. Imagining the aftermath of death, the piece embodies the view of a suicide victim's lover, taking place on London's tube network and following her fragmented thoughts. It is a piece about love, loss and the line between sanity and insanity.

Prior knowledge of the Kane play is not necessary to enjoy *Circles*, which has been described as 'graceful, passionate, emotive, soulful, honest' by audience members at its debut performance in 2012. A previous version has been published in the *Newhaven Journeyman*. Whilst the piece is fictional, the emotions and experiences are inspired by elements of my life, and it has been written with the aim of bringing comfort and healing to those who can relate to its themes.

Many thanks to the Burning Eye Books team for taking on this project, which has been bubbling away for a few years now. Thanks also to the audience members and readers of this book for your support in the journey of this publication.

Lightning Source UK Ltd.
Milton Keynes UK
UKHW022222231019
352159UK00001B/1/P

9 781911 570790